# A Stew for Egor's Mom

Written by F.R. Robinson

Illustrated by Scott Nash

"I think I'll make a stew," said Egor.

He put a pot on the stove.

"Aren't you nice," said Mom.

"Corn would be nice in a stew," said Egor.

Egor put the corn in the pot.

"Those pea pods would be nice," said Egor.
Egor put the pea pods in the pot.

"A box of rice would be yummy," said Egor.

Egor put the box in the pot.

"A rose would be nice for Mom," said Egor.
Egor put the rose in the pot.

"We'll need forks," said Egor.

Egor put the forks in the pot.

"A log in the fireplace would be nice," said Egor.
He put a log in the pot.

Egor carried the stew to Mom.

"I made a stew for you," said Egor.

"Aren't you nice!" said Mom.

"What's in the stew?" she asked.

"Corn, pea pods, a box of rice, a rose, forks, and a log," said Egor.

"Yum!" said Mom.

"That's just how I like it!"